BOREDOM FIGHTERS!

TIGHTROPE BOOKS INC. 2008, TORONTO

BOREDOM FIGHTERS!

EDITED BY PAOLA POLETTO AND JAKE KENNEDY

Tightrope Books
17 Greyton Crescent
Toronto, Ontario
Canada m6e 2g1
www.tightropebooks.com

Editor: Paola Poletto & Jake Kennedy
Copyeditor: Shirarose Wilensky
Typesetting: David Bigham
Cover design: David Bigham

Canada Council
for the Arts

Conseil des Arts
du Canada

ONTARIO ARTS COUNCIL
CONSEIL DES ARTS DE L'ONTARIO

Produced with the support of the Canada Council for the Arts, the Ontario Arts Council and the City of Toronto through the Toronto Arts Council.

PRINTED AND BOUND IN CANADA

Library and Archives Canada Cataloguing in Publication

    Boredom fighters / edited by Jake Kennedy and Paola Poletto.

Poems.
ISBN 978-0-9783351-5-1

    1. Boredom--Poetry. 2. Canadian poetry (English)--21st century.
I. Poletto, Paola, 1969- II. Kennedy, Jake, 1972-

PS8293.1.B67 2008   C811'.6080353   C2008-904880-6

Times New Boring is the name given to a contemporary non-proprietary class of demi-serif typefaces. The reverse italic style is designed to reflect a sense of recreational recline, with slope on the font's long extenders calculated as the average tilt coefficient of reclining chairs purchased in Canada between 1952 and 1993. Serifs are present only on the lower extremities of each letterform and have an upward slope, conveying the sense that each letter is, in the common vernacular, putting its feet up. The width of each letterform stroke is calculated based on the standard equation $W = \Sigma/\int (\infty)$ where W equals the width of the stroke, Σ equals the mean number of hours spent out of bed in an average 24-hour period and $\int$ equals the number of hours spent watching television during that same time period.

Portia Priegert

CONTENTS

INTRODUCTION

Hello. There are a few things that seem to pop for us:

1/ pushing comic graphics to excess (lots of bubbles, lots of booms and lots of non-words)

2/ overwhelmingly gendered perspectives and narratives

3/ politically engagement (we are thinking of the environment—all the time)

We were reading an article today written by psychologist Pierce J. Howard (Director of Research at the Centre for Applied Cognitive Studies), when two things struck us:

1/ "Moods are temporary. When an emotional state is permanent, as in continual sadness [or boredom—we're interchanging the mood], that is a trait, not a mood. Typically, such traits cannot be changed without pharmaceuticals, surgery or therapy."

He goes on to say that moods can be managed ... with a simple five minute outdoor walk, among other things (we need light, air, exercise, change of pace) ...

2/ Howard suggests that the probable cause of boredom is that a task is too easy.

If boredom becomes a trait, we surmised, then mothers smash sons with vacuum cleaners, schools soporificize students in greasy cafeterias, governments crush the rebellious with plasma screens. Strangely, it's the "easy task" that causes boredom and yet there is nothing more difficult to manage than having nothing to do. Of course, we believe it is obscene and unethical to be without "doings." Just yesterday we received a letter from a neo-Situationist who said, "I remind you both that 'Boredom is Counter-Revolutionary'." Thus we created "An Itemization[1]" in order to atone: man with fists in

---

[1] We are not bored with Google Image Search—not at all. Warily, and yet still too often, we type words into the search box and hope for art-magic. All the while, we suppose, we are adding dollars to the wallets of people we probably wouldn't like if we met them. Still, yesterday, we typed "b-o-r-e-d-o-m" and got some magic in return: four or five screens of tablet-images showing humans in various states of boredom. Does the desk that gives birth to the body which grow hands only to catch the falling head? And who immured all these women in cells of gleaming tile? Then, after documenting them all, we weren't sure whether balloons meant tediousness or cubicles meant liberty. All the same, we hope you are active or sloth-like in your kitchen, office, or warehouse. We hope you are full of life or lethargy. We hope you have what you need to keep feeling full, or not. We hope you are okay.

cheeks, man with head on desk, woman with broom, man draped over fence, man with zzz's for head, man in clouds with fist in cheek, woman with head between legs, two men dressed in Red Sox shirts and hats on public transit, cartoon man giving speech, man with straw hat raising hand, two people each with crossed arms sitting up in bed, man exiting a plane door, man with face in keyboard, woman digging an escape hole in her kitchen floor, man in silhouette walking under tank gun, diagram showing flow of anxiety, man walking on ruin wall, group of people with multi-coloured balloons, businessman holding coffee cup, girl holding soft blue dinosaur, photograph of the mountains of Cadore, Italy, woodcut with house and tree branch and noose, boy with head held in palms, beach scene with surf and emerald water, blurred figure in recliner, woman in dorm room wearing cat ears, man climbing tree, huge red flag saying no more boredom, man sleeping on couch, man and woman sitting on white steps, two people looking out at the sea at the stern of a boat, chart showing long periods of inactivity, two puppets peering around a door, three penguins underneath clouds, cartoon man in office looking out window, woman wearing apron drinking liquor in kitchen.

Anyway, with epigonic respect to Dada and concrete poetry—and with of-the-moment admiration for the graphic novel—we'd like to think (we do think!) we've collected something other. Beaulieu, Bök, Ngui, Morin, Tysdal, McKay, Gaze, Priegert, Pickering, Mancini, Laliberte, Fowles & Zuber, and Eckhoff are also flatlanders, mandalas, leg-chewers, leaf-shakers, dogs, televisions, bricks, calligraphy, typefaces, remote controls, emblems, tazers, lightning bolts, hotels, and sinking cities. All of them sticking intrepidly to an unwavering index to the hirsute gargoyle ear-well of boredom. Thus, only the most exhilarating and deathless community of boredom fighters around.

Inside, graphic doesn't always trump poetry and thus the ultimate tug of war is—in the most captivating sense—a real yawnyarn between word and image. We like images and we like words.

If you are bored, this is the playground. Plus, zzzzzzzzzz.

BOREDOM FIGHTERS!

CIVILIZATION IS A PROCESS FOR UNDERSTANDING HUMANITY

MARC NGUI

Civilisation
IS A PROCESS
for Understanding
HUMANITY

i'm Being COMMUNICATED to
by PEOPLE from the FUTURE,
EVERYTHING i SAY is
» TRUE. «

Listen to ME you
RIDICULOUS HUMANS -
WHAT the FUCK
are YOU DOING TO
our FUTURE!

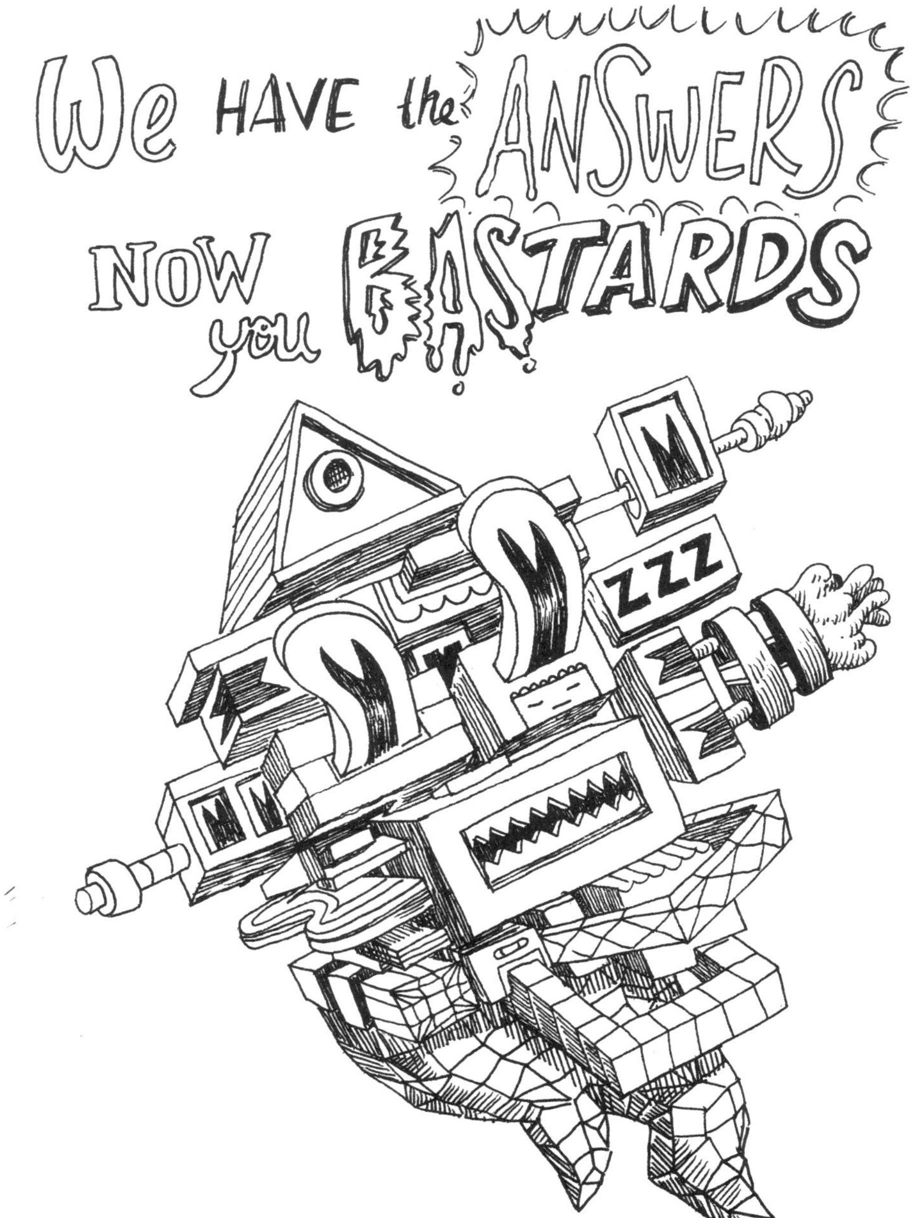
We HAVE the ANSWERS
NOW you BASTARDS
ZZZ

I'AM shaking like a LEAF

FLATLAND (5 EXCERPTS)

DEREK BEAULIEU

2

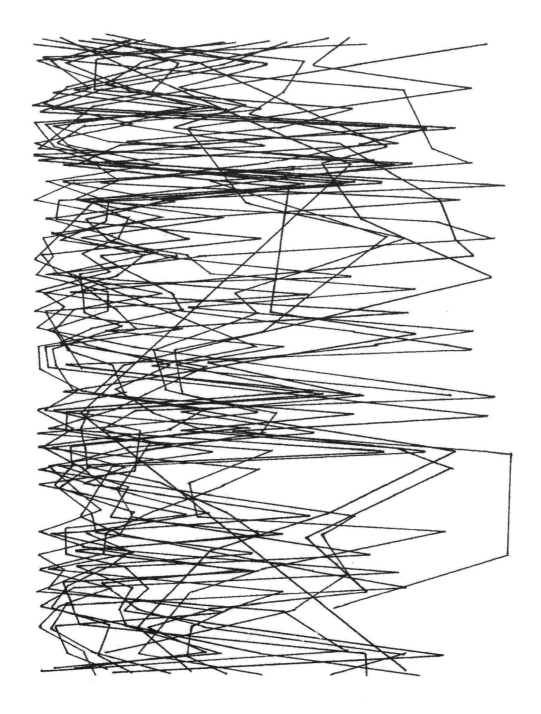

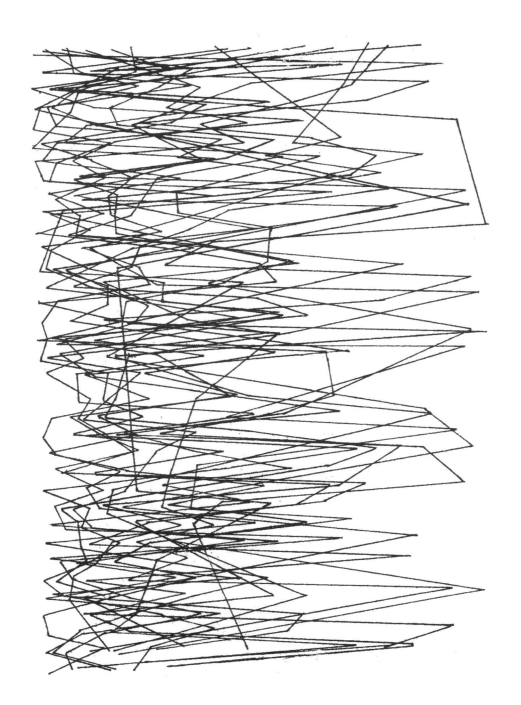

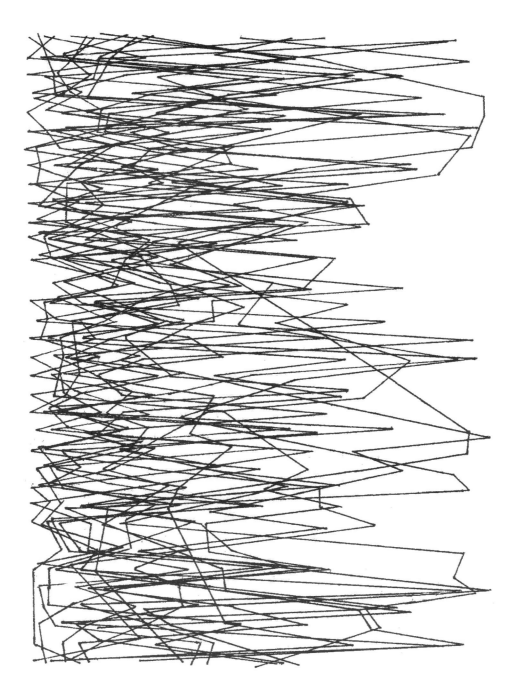

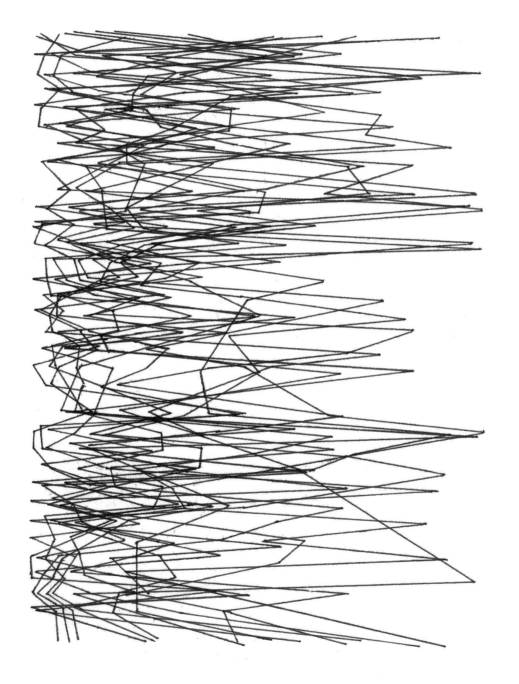

I AM DREAMING OF THE GRAND HOTEL EUROPE AGAIN (EXCERPT)

STACEY MAY FOWLES AND MARLENA ZUBER

7) **What do bodies decide?** Bodies are notorious for making faulty choices. Bodies tear and bleed, they bruise and bind and break, they are tied to bed frames and consumed, they conjure the most vicious of desires, the most vile aspects of animal will. Bodies do not write poetry or care of soul mates and magic. Bodies make Grand Hotel Europe reservations and lie and cheat and steal and leave scared and scarred.

Bodies fuck.

- must not think of < boy's name.>
   Taking a break.

MUMBLE GIRLS

KEVIN MCPHERSON ECKHOFF

4

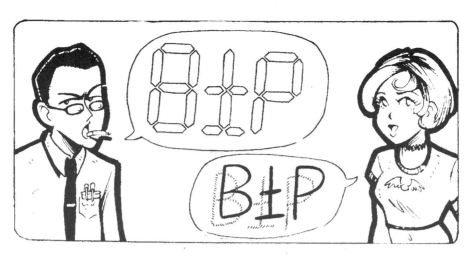

WHAT CAN A DOG DO?
PENULTIMATE QUESTION
GOODCOUNTRY STOCK

GUSTAVE MORIN

What can a dog do ? **paint, read, bark** What can a knife do ? **eat, cut, drink**

KITTEN CONSOMMÉ
LOUNGE ON ROOF
AT THE BEACH

PAOLA POLETTO

6

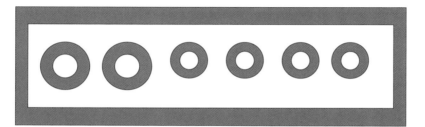

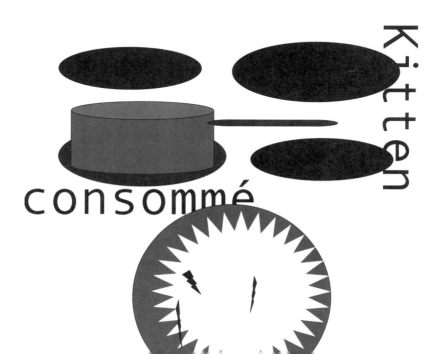

Kitten

consommé

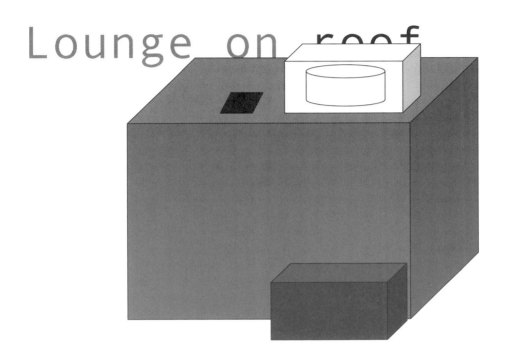

Lounge on roof

CUMULONIMBUS
SOUND POEM: BLOW-UP
STORM RECEDES

MARK LALIBERTE

7

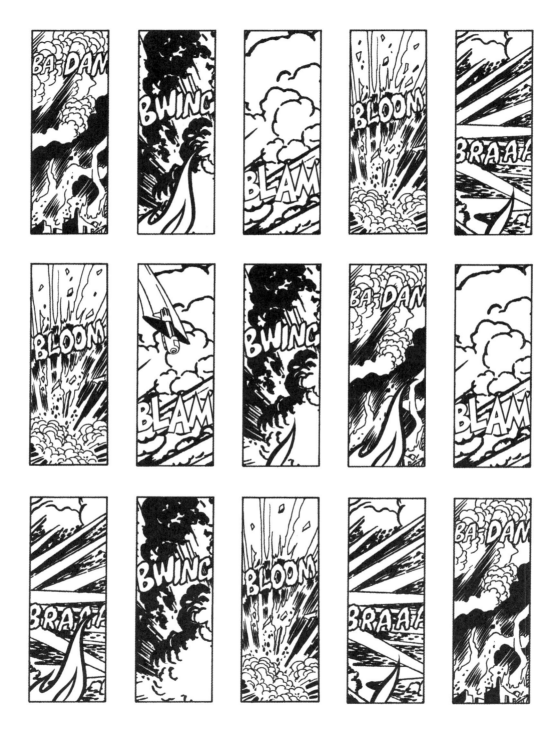

WHAT WOULD JESUS DRAW?

SHERWIN TJIA

SO PRETTY, AND THEY'RE ON EVERY WALL!

FIRST DAY BACK AND EVERYTHING IS CURIOUS, GORGEOUS AND ASTONISHING.

THESE AID HER TO SEE LONG DISTANCES!

THIS LITTLE NOTEBOOK ITSELF IS A MARVEL OF CONSTRUCTION.

PAINT! IN A CAN!

In case of loss, please return to:

As a Reward: $

THESE GREW UP THROUGH THE HARDEST OF STONE.

NOTEBOOK FOUND BY SHERWIN TJIA.

TODAY I JUST RODE BUSES. PEOPLE ARE SO CALM.

THE SPLAY OF THESE HANDS MADE ME WEEP REPEATEDLY.

WHILE NOT THE **GOOD** BOOK, STILL A GOOD BOOK.

REMINDS ME OF JOHN.

LUMINOUS.

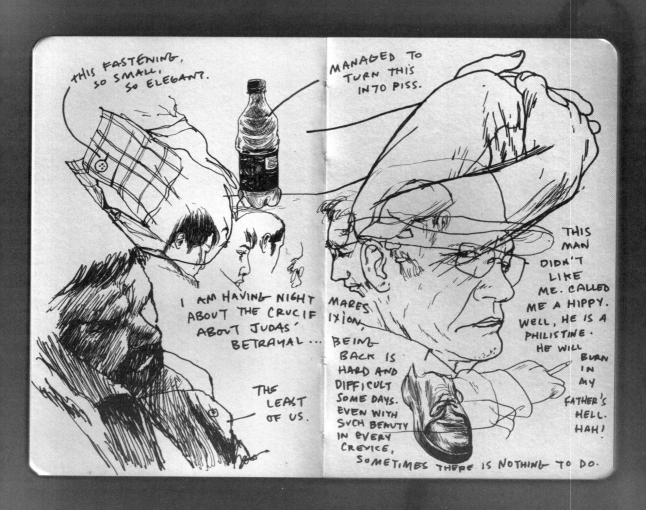

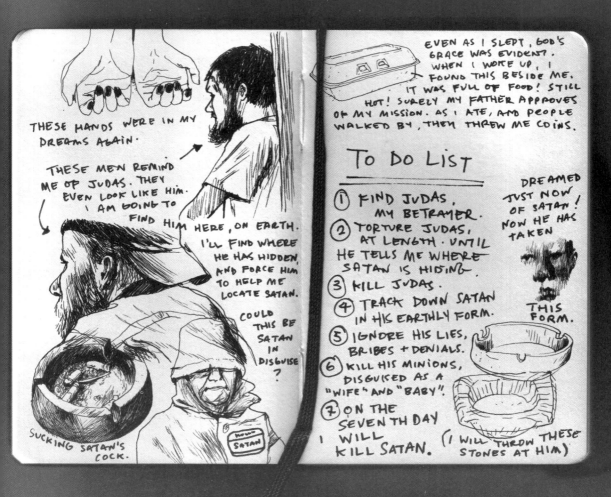

THESE HANDS WERE IN MY DREAMS AGAIN.

THESE MEN REMIND ME OF JUDAS. THEY EVEN LOOK LIKE HIM. I AM GOING TO FIND HIM HERE, ON EARTH.

I'LL FIND WHERE HE HAS HIDDEN, AND FORCE HIM TO HELP ME LOCATE SATAN.

COULD THIS BE SATAN IN DISGUISE?

SUCKING SATAN'S COCK.

EVEN AS I SLEPT, GOD'S GRACE WAS EVIDENT. WHEN I WOKE UP, I FOUND THIS BESIDE ME. IT WAS FULL OF FOOD! STILL HOT! SURELY MY FATHER APPROVES OF MY MISSION. AS I ATE, AND PEOPLE WALKED BY, THEY THREW ME COINS.

TO DO LIST

1. FIND JUDAS, MY BETRAYER.
2. TORTURE JUDAS, AT LENGTH. UNTIL HE TELLS ME WHERE SATAN IS HIDING.
3. KILL JUDAS.
4. TRACK DOWN SATAN IN HIS EARTHLY FORM.
5. IGNORE HIS LIES, BRIBES + DENIALS.
6. KILL HIS MINIONS, DISGUISED AS A "WIFE" AND "BABY".
7. ON THE SEVENTH DAY I WILL KILL SATAN. (I WILL THROW THESE STONES AT HIM)

DREAMED JUST NOW OF SATAN! NOW HE HAS TAKEN

THIS FORM.

SERGEANT DEADHEAD, THE ASTRONUT!

DANIEL SCOTT TYSDAL

10. Last Words (Though Not from Outerspace)

Sent to Murder the Moon, but Murdered by It Moon Mission
Aborted! MoonMan Still Missing! "True last words,"
National Authorities taught, "can be nothing more than victorious headlines
you will not survive to read." Possessing an operational
Tele-Disseminator (, , or), our MoonMan could at best be salvaged
as an interview that would end with the line: MoonMan Says:
"The Rule of the Moon Is Different Up Close" "Up close,"
as his Master warned, "there is room for disbelief

in moon. Up close its given name is as unmemorable as sleeping early
when we had hoped to wake late." `MoonMan's Body`
`Recovered!` is the only declaration he allows the future of the forces
that resigned him to extinguish a single glint of sky's residing
shine—

the only
poems his rescuers
will rescue here
are
these:

"In
Uniform
and
Posing
with Firearm (during graduation)"

"Side
of
House (in
civies just
days before

lifting-

off)"

9. On His Master's Escape

One year before the mission, while our MoonMan was still in training, his
Master was exiled for asking the class to ask the question: "does the moon
inflict our suffering or reflect our sent suffering back?" His Master had refused
to teach "one more batch of Astro*nuts* that the moon was nothing more than a
reminder of our failure to destroy the moon . . . does not deserve a spot in our
stock of dirty words . . . no to missile-choked plots . . . protest . . . psalm . . . ."

Our MoonMan's Master left an address (Somewhere in the Difference / between
Mission / and Ritual, between / Operation and / Ceremony) and a last lesson:

contemplate the duty of sea names for a sea surface
with no sea spray, sea birds,
sea

8. Recollection of Graduatio

n day. Five years after the undertaken training finished, our MoonMan
and his MoonMates were done; and during their first few winks of relief (to

gether) they discussed

who they were
fighting
for,

What it
does
to
memories.

the
moon's
vilest
traits,

their most
terrible
fears

, their plans
for the
future   after

of
war,
with no idea
that in days an Agent
of the Moon would claim everyone
in this photograph
but him(   ).

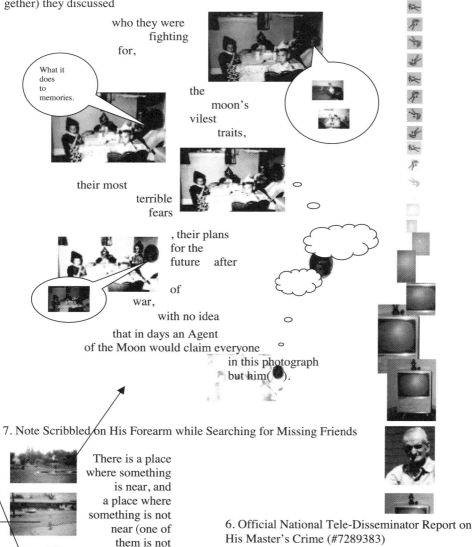

7. Note Scribbled on His Forearm while Searching for Missing Friends

There is a place
where something
is near, and
a place where
something is not
near (one of
them is not
the moon and

6. Official National Tele-Disseminator Report on
His Master's Crime (#7289383)

This just in.
After an
intensive and well-

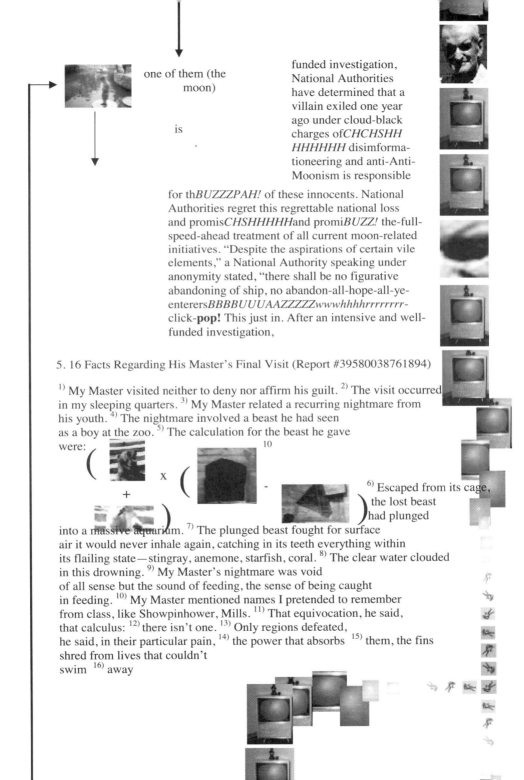

one of them (the moon)

is

.

funded investigation, National Authorities have determined that a villain exiled one year ago under cloud-black charges of *CHCHSHH HHHHHH* disimformationeering and anti-Anti-Moonism is responsible

for th*BUZZZPAH!* of these innocents. National Authorities regret this regrettable national loss and promis*CHSHHHHH*and promi*BUZZ!* the-full-speed-ahead treatment of all current moon-related initiatives. "Despite the aspirations of certain vile elements," a National Authority speaking under anonymity stated, "there shall be no figurative abandoning of ship, no abandon-all-hope-all-ye-enterers*BBBBUUUAAZZZZZwwwhhhhrrrrrrr*-click-**pop!** This just in. After an intensive and well-funded investigation,

5. 16 Facts Regarding His Master's Final Visit (Report #39580038761894)

[1] My Master visited neither to deny nor affirm his guilt. [2] The visit occurred in my sleeping quarters. [3] My Master related a recurring nightmare from his youth. [4] The nightmare involved a beast he had seen as a boy at the zoo. [5] The calculation for the beast he gave were:

[6] Escaped from its cage, the lost beast had plunged into a massive aquarium. [7] The plunged beast fought for surface air it would never inhale again, catching in its teeth everything within its flailing state—stingray, anemone, starfish, coral. [8] The clear water clouded in this drowning. [9] My Master's nightmare was void of all sense but the sound of feeding, the sense of being caught in feeding. [10] My Master mentioned names I pretended to remember from class, like Showpinhower, Mills. [11] That equivocation, he said, that calculus: [12] there isn't one. [13] Only regions defeated, he said, in their particular pain, [14] the power that absorbs [15] them, the fins shred from lives that couldn't swim [16] away

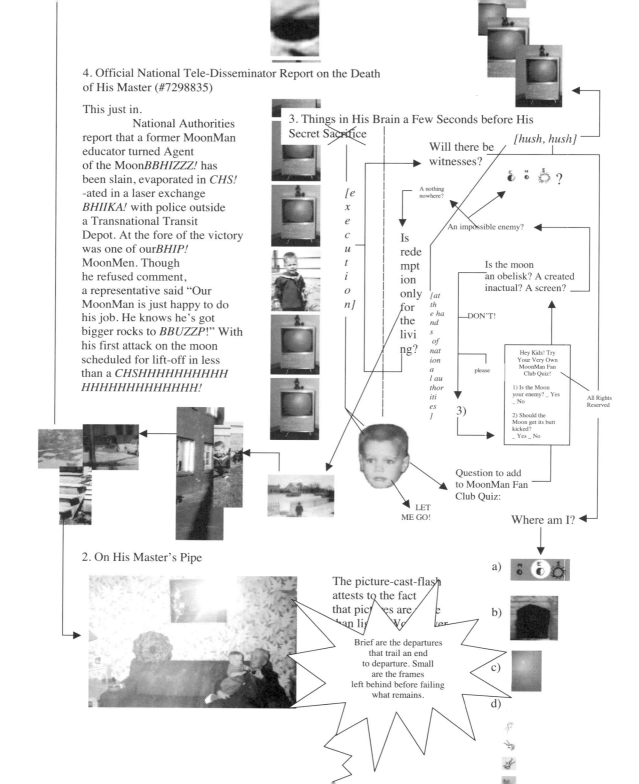

4. Official National Tele-Disseminator Report on the Death of His Master (#7298835)

This just in.
National Authorities report that a former MoonMan educator turned Agent of the Moon*BBHIZZZ!* has been slain, evaporated in *CHS!*-ated in a laser exchange *BHIIKA!* with police outside a Transnational Transit Depot. At the fore of the victory was one of our*BHIP!* MoonMen. Though he refused comment, a representative said "Our MoonMan is just happy to do his job. He knows he's got bigger rocks to *BBUZZP*!" With his first attack on the moon scheduled for lift-off in less than a *CHSHHHHHHHHHH HHHHHHHHHHHHH!*

3. Things in His Brain a Few Seconds before His Secret Sacrifice

[hush, hush]

Will there be witnesses?

[execution]

[at the hands of national authorities]

Is redemption only for the living?

A nothing nowhere?

An impossible enemy?

Is the moon an obelisk? A created inactual? A screen?

DON'T!

please

3)

ᵇ ? ?

Hey Kids! Try Your Very Own MoonMan Fan Club Quiz!

1) Is the Moon your enemy? _ Yes _ No

2) Should the Moon get its butt kicked? _ Yes _ No

Question to add to MoonMan Fan Club Quiz:

LET ME GO!

Where am I?

a)

b)

c)

d)

2. On His Master's Pipe

The picture-cast-flash attests to the fact that pictures are [...] [...]an li[...] [...]

Brief are the departures that trail an end to departure. Small are the frames left behind before failing what remains.

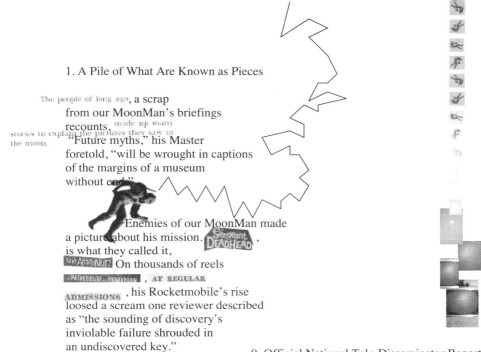

1. A Pile of What Are Known as Pieces

The people of long ago, a scrap
from our MoonMan's briefings
recounts, made up many
stories to explain the pictures they saw in
the moon. "Future myths," his Master
foretold, "will be wrought in captions
of the margins of a museum
without end."

Enemies of our MoonMan made
a picture about his mission. SERGEANT DEADHEAD ,
is what they called it,
THE ASTRONUT On thousands of reels
"PATHECOLOR"...FANTSCOPE , AT REGULAR

ADMISSIONS , his Rocketmobile's rise
loosed a scream one reviewer described
as "the sounding of discovery's
inviolable failure shrouded in
an undiscovered key."

0. Official National Tele-Disseminator Report
on the Recovery of His Corpse (#7300590)

This just in

TIME TRAVEL

SALLY MCKAY

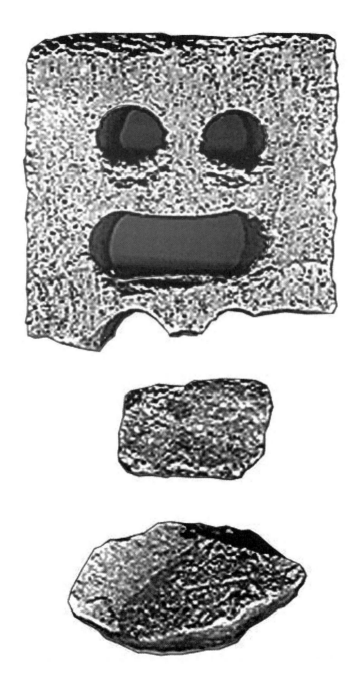

ASEMIC POEM

TIM GAZE

HAIL

DONATO MANCINI

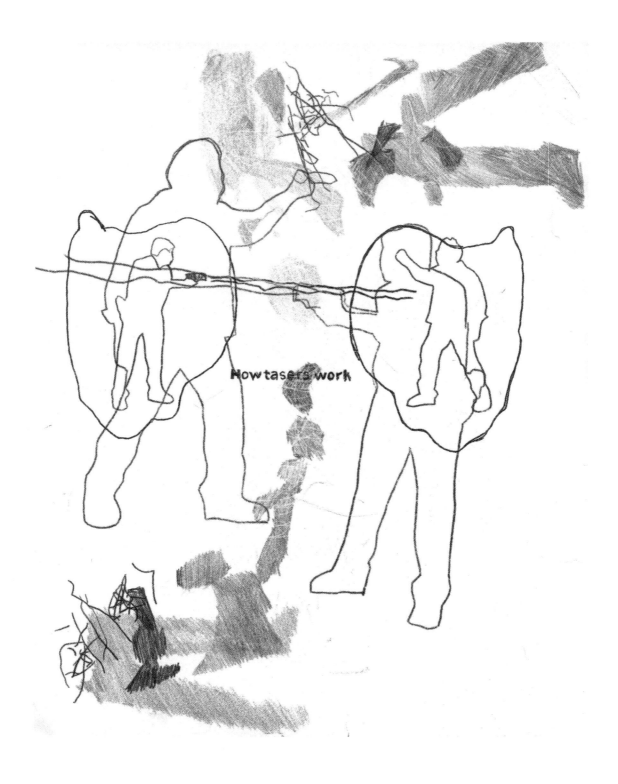

How tasers work

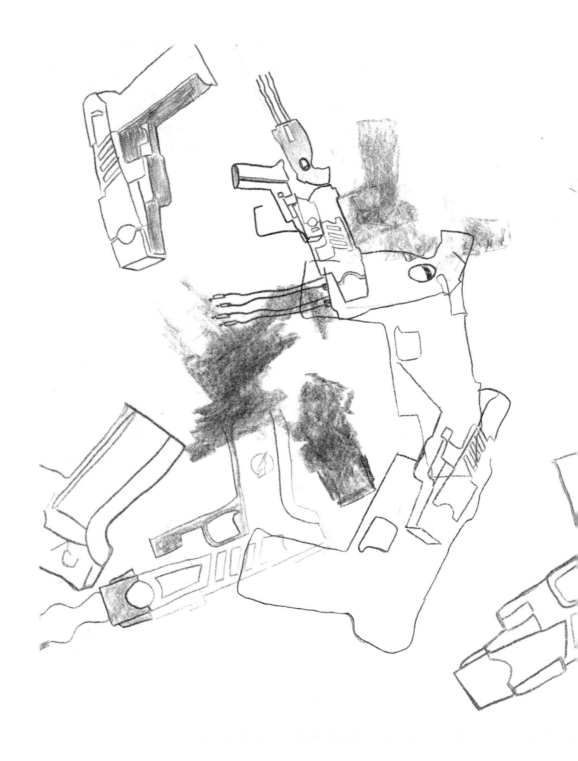

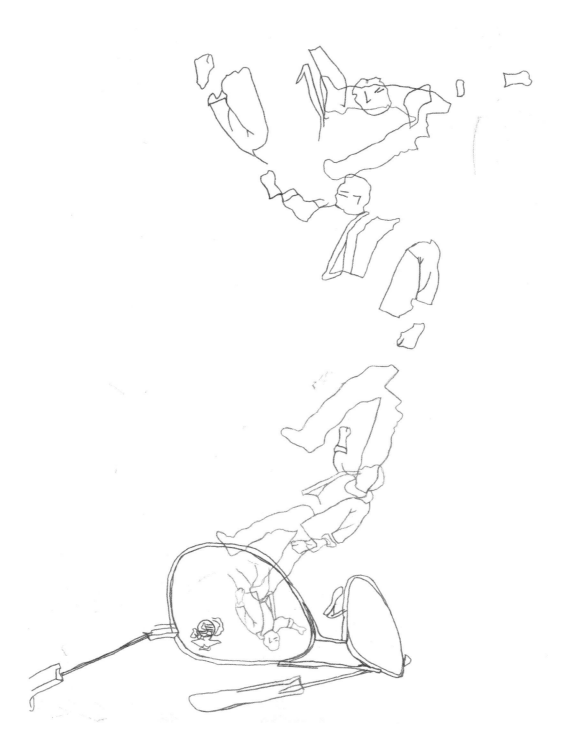

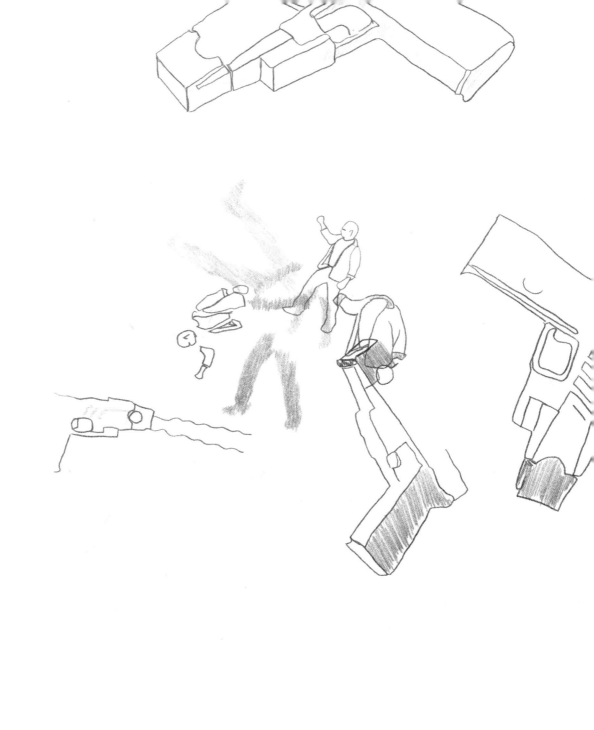

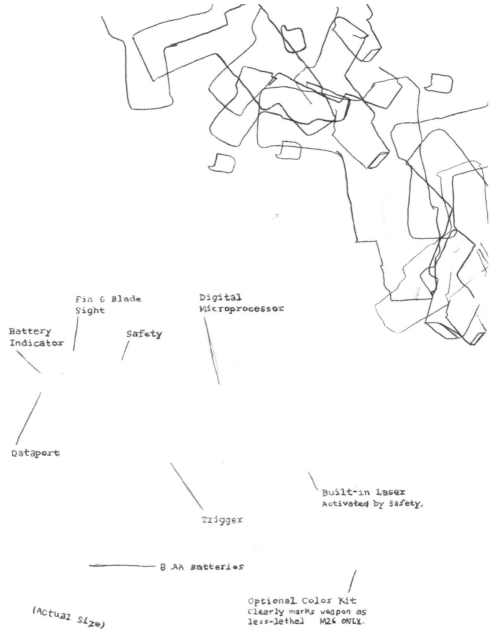

Battery
Indicator

Fin & Blade
Sight

Safety

Digital
Microprocessor

Dataport

Built-in Laser
Activated by safety.

Trigger

8 AA Batteries

(Actual Size)

Optional Color Kit
Clearly marks weapon as
less-lethel   M26 ONLY.

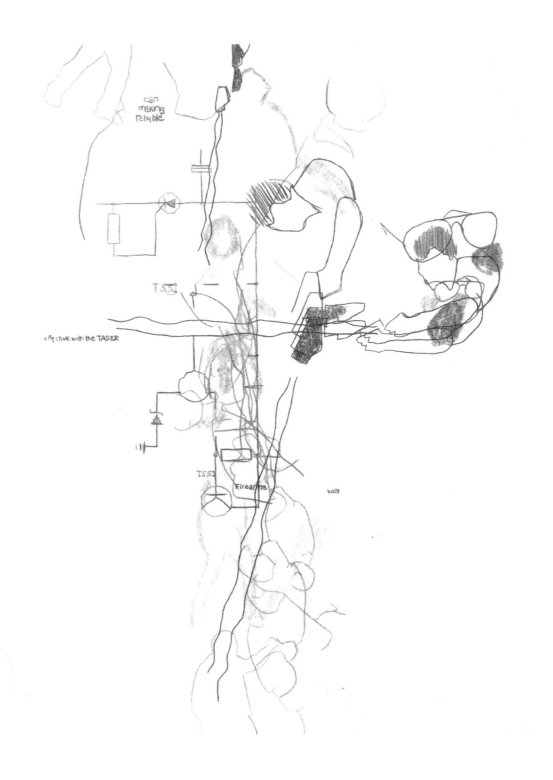

can
making
reimble

TSSI

effective with the TASER

TSSI

Firearms   body

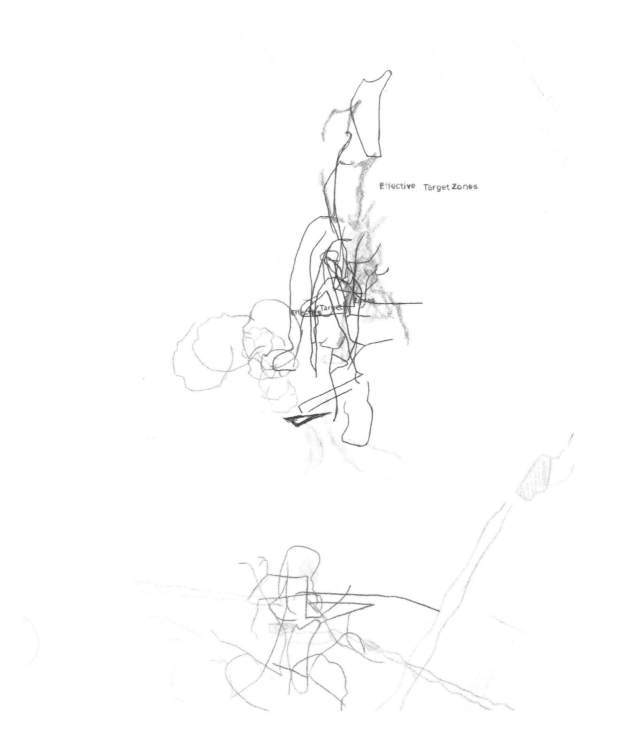

Effective Target Zones

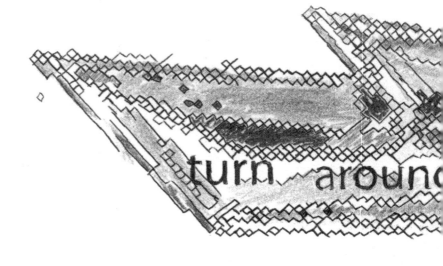

, bright eyes

REMOTE

JENNIFER PICKERING

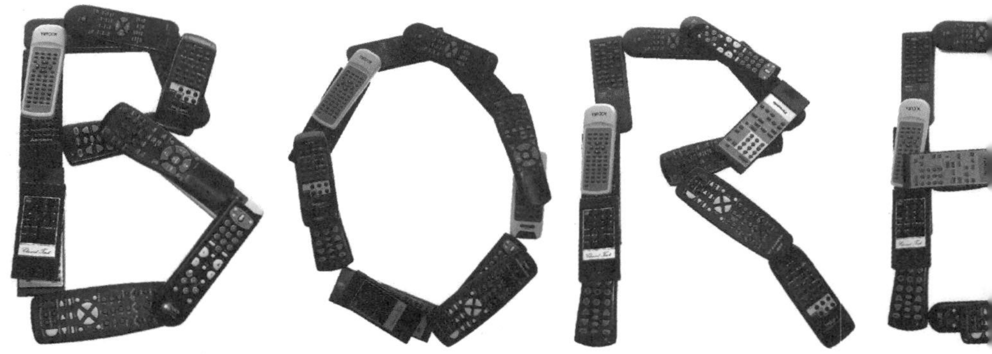

SIMPLEX CRYSTAL (GROWTH IN PROGRESS)

CHRISTIAN BÖK

14

KING: DEEDS AND SUFFERING
STUDIES IN MICRO-SCANSION II: EXCLAMATION TOWER
STUDIES IN MICRO-SCANSION III: PINNA OF SEMI-COLONIZATION
STUDIES IN MICRO-SCANSION IV: MORPHOLOGY OF A UNIVALVE PERIOD.
FIG. 23A PUNCTUATION FOSSIL
THE STARS, HE SAID.

GARY BARWIN

15

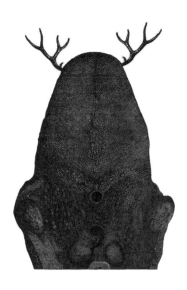

Studies in Micro-Scansion II: Exclamation Tower

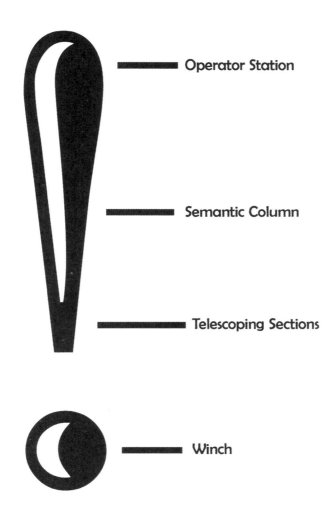

Operator Station

Semantic Column

Telescoping Sections

Winch

Studies in Micro-Scansion III: Pinna of Semi-Colonization

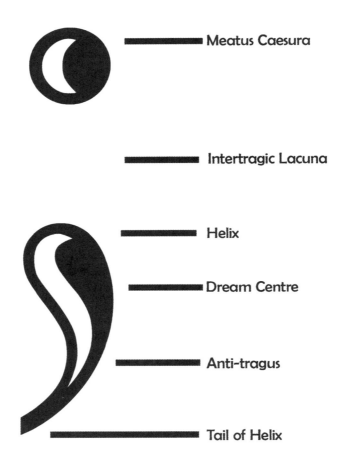

Meatus Caesura

Intertragic Lacuna

Helix

Dream Centre

Anti-tragus

Tail of Helix

Studies in Micro-Scansion IV: Morphology of a Univalve Period.

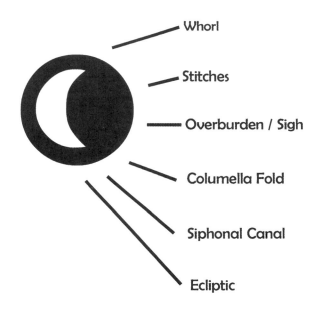

Whorl

Stitches

Overburden / Sigh

Columella Fold

Siphonal Canal

Ecliptic

Absent:

Spent Fuel Storage Bay
Endoplasmic Reticulum

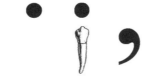

Fig. 23a Punctuation Fossil

The stars, he said.

LEGEND

JAKE KENNEDY

16

Legend

They moved east into the sun.

They watched the wind.

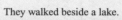

They walked beside a lake.

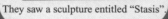

They saw a sculpture entitled "Stasis".

They heard him approach.

He was a snake, gasping.

They refused to return.

He got mad, madder, maddest.

They counted seconds for many years.

SUPERBOY

PAUL HONG AND BEN J. FREY

SUPERBOY

Written by Paul Hong
Illustrated by Ben Frey

ENDNOTES

King: Deeds and Suffering
Studies in Micro-Scansion II: Exclamation Tower
Fig. 23a Punctuation Fossil
Studies in Micro-Scansion III: Pinna of Semi-Colonization
Studies in Micro-Scansion IV: Morphology of a Univalve Period
and *The stars, he said*

by Gary Barwin

Not making sense, waging sense. What are the limits of A? Of H? Green. Blue. Blue-green. Say E with the lips. U with the tongue. Think of T. If we were not symmetrical — arms, legs, face — would the letters be different? What if we had three mouths or two tongues? If our tongues were forked? If we could speak from other orifices? With other animals? If we were blind and had no fingertips? The whales' alphabet. The alphabet of owls. The vowels of the ptarmigan. The letters of the tarmac. Each tree is an alphabet. Or each tree is a single letter. Can't pronounce the forest for the trees. Each car is an alphabet. Or each car is a single letter. Can't read the traffic for the destination. If we invented computers before letters? If there was a limit on the number of letters we could have? If letters changed meaning? If letters became extinct? If we had to have a public advocacy campaign to support certain letters? If you needed a licence for certain letters or proper training? How do we make the alphabet global? Could there be different letters for the left handed? Print. Cursive. Something else. How do we address the three dimensions of the alphabet? What are the most beloved letters? What should we do on the national holiday for letters? Not making sounds. Waging sounds. Not making words. Waging words. Not making sense. Waging sense. What if different corporations bought advertising space on the letters? What if they bought the letters? What if we ceased to see the letters but rather the corporation? Can't see the forest for the ads. What if the letters were copyrighted? Taxed? Made illegal? How do we apologize for the alphabet? How do we atone for it? How can it bring us new joy?

Flatland

by derek beaulieu

These excerpts are from a page-by-page response to E.A. Abbott's *Flatland*, a Victorian science-fiction satirical novel which posits a two-dimensional universe inhabited entirely by polygons.

For each page of Abbott's novel I traced, by hand, a system which distances "writing" from a creative act into one of boring, rote production, a representation of each letter's occurrence across every page of text. The generated result is a series of superimposed seismographic images which reduce the text in question into a two-dimensional schematic reminiscent of EKG results or stock reports.

This project builds upon my previous work in poetry, and a theorizing of a briefly non-signifying poetic, where the graphic mark of text becomes fore-grounded both as a rhizomatic map of possibility, and as a record of authorial movement.

Much as the Victorian novel A Human Document, gives rise to Tom Phillips' ongoing graphic interpretation A Humument, Flatland has resulted in a book-length interpretation of the graphic possibilities of a text without text. Derrida, writing on Blanchot, asked "How can one text, assuming its unity, give or present another to be read, without touching it, without saying anything about it, practically without referring to it?" Each page of my graphically-realized Flatland is a completely unique, diagrammatic representation of the occurrences of letters. By reducing reading and language to a paragrammatical statistical analysis, content is subsumed into graphical representation of how language covers a page. Flatland attempts to flatten the plane of text.

Simplex Crystal (Growth in Progress)

by Christian Bök

A Letraset mandala that, so far, exhausts all the letters made of straight lines on a single sheet of type.

Asemic Poem

by Tim Gaze

A magician casts a spell upon himself, in order to escape the stasis of boredom. It looks like writing, but we can't quite read it. I call works like this "asemic writing."

Asemic writing has been made by poets, writers, painters, calligraphers, children, and scribblers all around the world. Most people make asemic writing at some time, possibly when testing a new pen. Educators talk about children going through distinct stages of "mock letters," "pseudowriting," and so on, when they're learning to write. Many of us made asemic writing before we were able to write words. Looking at asemic writing does something to us. Some examples have pictograms or ideograms, which suggest a meaning through their shape. Others take us for a ride along their curves. We like some, we dislike others.

Time Travel

by Sally McKay

1 Killer Whales

Killer Whales are like an abstract thought; so wild and indifferent, so huge and cruel and overwhelming. But they are also tragic. Their impending doom signifies an end of days, one that is wrought by the relentless, stupid progress of humanity rather than by any divine design. As a symbol, the killer whale is both outside of us and of us, in a way that signifies our abject failure to relate with the natural world. Maybe there would be hope if bio-science could find a way to interbreed our species. Presently we stumble around, sticking killer whales into big fish tanks, teaching them cute and fumbling tricks. If only we could relinquish our genome and join them in the seas.

2 Kinds of Brick-Person

This spread depicts human time travel in both directions, as well as in lateral shifts; the kind of time travel that takes place in human consciousness. In the future there is nothing left but clean fill and old stones, rocks that predate bricks by thousands, if not millions, of years. In the past were creatures who resembled humans and shared many of our characteristics. We dig them up and wonder about their motivations. In the present we think of everything and furiously make images to tease and entertain the eye.

3 Birds

Our colossal failure as custodians of this planet is in a tautological spiral. We want what we can't have so we render it and own it and destroy it. But bird song is not music, and the Red-winged Blackbirds in our hedges, fields, and swampy ditches don't care a whit for our bird books or museums.

Mumble Girls

by kevin mcpherson eckhoff

These pieces re-imagine the onomatopoeic language from Lea Hernandez's comic, *Rumble Girls*, as dialogue in the Unifon script used throughout the original text to indicate corporate ownership.

Kitten consommé, Lounge on roof, and At the beach

by Paola Poletto

These are some of my dreams. I reconstruct a dream narrative using a standardized palette of shapes, or symbols, to create one poem that I do not wholly own or understand, from a dream I do not wholly own or understand. Drawing and writing from dreams was a Surrealist strategy that has always appealed to me. It was like losing control, in a very controlled sort of way. Capturing my dreams with *Drawing AutoShapes* in Microsoft Word is getting at something that makes me slightly uneasy, almost giddy.

Legend

by Jake Kennedy

The images in this piece are taken from a single card of a German boardgame entitled Verkehrs-Lotto. I found the game at a Value Village in Kelowna, BC. I enjoy the process of taking an existing text or, in this case, a set of images and applying some gentle redirection. So "Legend," on one level, tries to find the poetry and narrative tension otherwise concealed in traffic signs. More specifically it hints at the story of my fraternal grandmother who was forced to flee with her children from an abusive husband.

CONTRIBUTORS

Gary Barwin Writer, composer, and performer, Gary Barwin lives in Hamilton, Ontario. His books include *frogments from the frag pool* (poetry; with derek beaulieu), *Doctor Weep and Other Strange Teeth* (fiction), *Raising Eyebrows* (poetry) and *Outside the Hat* (poetry). A new book of poetry, is forthcoming from Coach House. He can be found at garybarwin.com and serifofnottingblog.blogspot.com.

derek beaulieu is the author, or co-author, of five books of poetry, including *fractal economies* (Talon Books, Vancouver) and *Flatland* (information as material, York, UK). He is also co-editor of *Shift & Switch: New Canadian poetry*. His work has been shown and published internationally.

Christian Bök is the author not only of *Crystallography* (Coach House Books, 1994), a pataphysical encyclopedia nominated for the Gerald Lampert Memorial Award, but also of *Eunoia* (Coach House Books, 2001), a bestselling work of experimental literature, which has gone on to win the Griffin Prize for Poetic Excellence. Bök has created artificial languages for two television shows: *Gene Roddenberry's Earth: Final Conflict* and *Peter Benchley's Amazon*. Bök has also earned many accolades for his virtuoso performances of sound poetry (particularly the *Ursonate* by Kurt Schwitters). His conceptual artworks (which include books built out of Rubik's cubes and Lego bricks) have appeared at the Marianne Boesky Gallery in New York City as part of the exhibit *Poetry Plastique*. Bök is currently a Professor of English at the University of Calgary.

kevin mcpherson eckhoff recently completed an MA in English literature, with a focus on creative writing, at the University of Calgary. He is the author of five poetry chapbooks, including *Signs of divorce* (Canadian Poetry Association, 2006), which co-won the 2005 Shaunt Basmajian Chapbook Award, & most recently *Gordian Denouement* (No Press, 2007). His work appears in the anthologies, *Decalogue Three: Ten Visual Poets* (Chaudière, 2008) and *Outside Voices 2008 Anthology of Younger Poets* (Outside Voices Press, 2008), as well as previous or forthcoming issues of *Open Letter*, *Filling station*, *Descant*, *Spell,* and *Offerta Speciale*. Residing with his delightful partner Laurel in BC, kevin, in his spare time, teaches at Okanagan College.

CONTRIBUTORS

Stacey May Fowles' written work has been published in various magazines and journals, including *Shameless Magazine, Kiss Machine,* and *subTERRAIN.* Her non-fiction writing has been anthologized in the widely acclaimed *Nobody Passes: Rejecting the Rules of Gender and Conformity and First Person Queer.* She is collaborating on a graphic novel with artist Marlena Zuber and her first novel, *Be Good,* is currently out with Tightrope Books.

Ben Frey has been a freelance illustrator and artist since graduating from design school in 2007. Being a resident of the Olympics-obsessed city of Vancouver, Ben has spent most of last year living in Berlin, inspired by the big art scene there. He is back in Vancouver and is currently illustrating his second children's book for Annick Press that is due to be on shelves in spring 2009.

Tim Gaze is chasing the slippery creature named Writing where it leads him. His fiction, poetry, essays and asemic compositions have been published all over the place. One of his sources of inspiration is music, particularly African & Jamaican rhythms. He lives in the Adelaide Hills, South Australia.

Paul Hong is the author of *Your Love is Murder or the Case of the Mangled Pie.* He lives in Toronto.

Jake Kennedy teaches creative writing and English literature at Okanagan College. Please send him electronic mail: jakedavidkennedy@gmail.com

Mark Laliberte (b. 1971) makes art and artist multiples, curates exhibitions, and designs books, books, more books ... he is currently the Managing Editor of both *Carousel* and *Descant* magazines. Laliberte recently began teaching Publications: Print at the Ontario College of Art and Design, Toronto. Info: marklaliberte.com, popnoir.ca, carouselmagazine.ca

Donato Mancini is the author of two books of visual poetry, *Ligatures* (New Star Books, 2005) and *Æthel* (New Star Books, 2007). Other parts of "Hail" have appeared as no. 22 in the *Hell Passport* chapbook series published by Perro Verlag, and in the visual poetry anthology *Decalogue 3.*

Sally McKay, is an artist working in performance, video, and digital art. She is also an independent curator, a writer and an editor. Sally is engaged in a long-term project about perception, science, and wilderness, which includes a multi-media project about neutrinos, *The Trouble With Oscillation*, presented as part of the touring group show, *Neutrinos They Are Very Small*. She was co-owner/editor of the Toronto art magazine Lola, and she currently writes a column on art and science for *Kiss Machine*. McKay recently curated the touring show *Quantal Strife* for Doris McCarthy Gallery UTSC, Toronto (2006), and *Mods and Rockers, digifest* and Harbourfront Centre, Toronto (2006). She recently curated the Kitchener Waterloo Art Gallery's 2007 Biennial.

gustave morin is a werewolf and a ferris wheel, the demon-barber of concrete in Canada, the maker of a "few poetry," and the author of some five books in and out of print, most recently *The Etcetera Barbecue* (BookThug, 2006) and *A Penny Dreadful* (2003, pulped).

Marc Ngui (b. 1972, Guyana) is a cartoonist and diagrammatician whose work is firmly rooted in DIY culture. He figures he is on a lifelong exploration into the mechanics of visual communication as a means of processing information and emotional experience. As a freelancer he has worked in illustration, comics, storyboards, animation, video journalism, exhibition design, sign painting, maps, diagrams, pictograms, and icons. More information about his work can be found at www.bumblenut.com.

Jennifer Pickering was born in Lausanne, Switzerland, and raised in Canada in the Okanagan Valley. Pickering is a visual artist and a graduate from the MFA studio arts program at the University of British Columbia. Her work has been exhibited at various solo and group exhibitions in BC. Jennifer was also a participant in the *Free Manifesta, Manifesta 4* in Frankfurt, Germany.

Paola Poletto is an artist coordinator. Her work includes program direction for Design Exchange and co-founder of *Kiss Machine* before joining the Office of Arts and Culture of Mississauga. She is curator of *Fashion no no*, an exhibition exploring the relationship between art, design, and craft (Harbourfront Centre, Toronto, January 2009). Her art has been exhibited at various group exbitions in Canada, the US, and Europe. She may be reached at paolapoletto@gmail.com.

CONTRIBUTORS

Portia Priegert is an artist and writer based in Kelowna, BC. She is currently subjecting herself to a disciplined protocol of reruns and web surfing in an effort to determine whether boredom is a finite or infinite construct.

Sherwin Tjia has written four books and illustrated two. One of them, *The World is a Heartbreaker*, was a finalist for the A.M. Klein Award for Poetry. These days he organizes Slowdance Nights, complete with condom corsages, dancecards, and designated dancers.

Daniel Scott Tysdal received the 2007 ReLit Award, the 2006 Anne Szumigalski Poetry Award, and the 2004 John V. Hicks Manuscript Award for his first book of poetry, *Predicting the Next Big Advertising Breakthrough Using a Potentially Dangerous Method*. He currently lives in Toronto.

Marlena Zuber is an illustrator and artist. She does editorial illustrations for various magazines and will shortly be commencing her first graphic novel with author Stacey May Fowles. Marlena makes maps for Toronto projects like *murmur*. She works at Creative Works Studio, and is a member of the band *Tomboyfriend*.

BOREDOM FIGHTERS!

Thank you Halli Villegas! for approaching us with your
curiosity in graphic poetry, and for letting us dream up
this book.

Paola and Jake